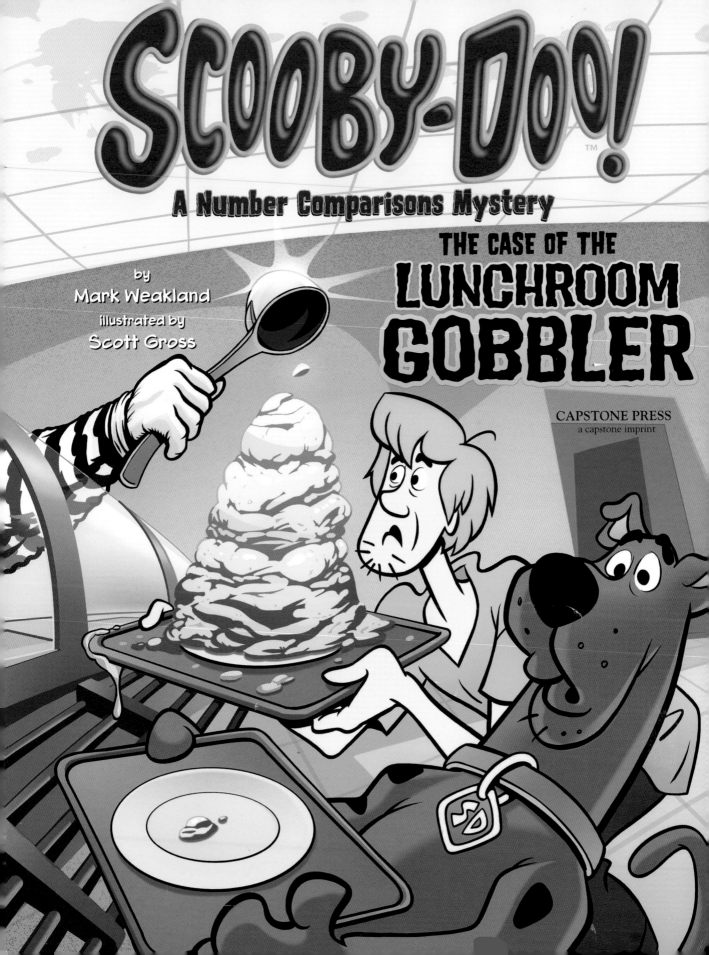

Published in 2015 by Capstone Press
A Capstone Imprint
1710 Roe Crest Drive
North Mankato, Minnesota 56003
www.capstonepub.com

CAPS32483

Library of Congress Cataloging-in-Publication Data
Weakland, Mark, author.
Scooby-Doo! a number comparisons mystery : the case of the lunchroom gobbler /
by Mark Weakland ; illustrated by Scott Gross.
pages cm. — (Solve it with Scooby-Doo! : math)
Summary: "The popular Scooby-Doo and the Mystery Inc. gang teach kids all about number
comparisons"— Provided by publisher.
Audience: Age 5-7.
Audience: Grades K to 3.
ISBN 978-1-4914-1542-9 (library binding)
1. Number concept—Juvenile literature. 2. Scooby-Doo (Fictitious character)—Juvenile
literature. I. Gross, Scott, illustrator. II. Title. III. Title: Case of the lunchroom gobbler.

QA141.3.W429 2015
512.7—dc23   2014001831

Editor: Shelly Lyons
Designer: Lori Bye
Art Director: Nathan Gassman
Production Specialist: Charmaine Whitman
The illustrations in this book were created digitally.

Thanks to our adviser for his expertise, research, and advice:
Jean B. Nganou, PhD
Department of Mathematics
University of Oregon

Printed in the United States of America in North Mankato, Minnesota.
032015   008793R

The kids at Crystal Cove High School were confused. The cafeteria food portions had always been the same. But recently the portions were never equal. What could be happening?

Scooby-Doo and the gang got to the school just in time for lunch. "I'm hungry," said Shaggy. "Let's get some eats." They stood in line with their trays.

4 < 7

5 > 2

Let's look for clues.

The gang went to the place where the food had been made. There they found plates with **4** pretzels and **7** pretzels. They also found plates of **8** grapes and **12** grapes.

Daphne began to match up the food.

13

Scooby and Shaggy walked the halls. They passed the library and the gym. Outside the art room, they saw things on the floor.

Raftey rin!

"Yep, a safety pin and a black magic marker," said Shaggy.

Just then a gray shape swooped out of the gym.

Shaggy and Scooby took off running toward the cafeteria. The gobbler was not far behind.

Scooby and Shaggy slid around the corner and hid. Fred put the bread into the toaster and pushed the button. Soon black smoke was pouring out.

"Fire!" yelled Shaggy
The gobbler ran for the exit.

"Good grief!" said Principal Nicklebee. "It's Vivian Tatertot, the head lunch lady! And her gobbler costume is missing a safety pin."

"That's right," said Velma, "And she used the black magic marker to color her clothing!"

Glossary

equal—being the same in number; the sign for "equal to" is =

greater than—being larger in number; the sign for "greater than" is ⟩

investigate—to check to find out something

less than—being smaller in number; the sign for "less than" is ⟨

meddling—busying oneself with something that is not one's concern

Internet Sites

FactHound offers a safe, fun way to find Internet sites related to this book. All of the sites on FactHound have been researched by our staff.

Here's all you do:

Visit www.facthound.com

Type in this code: 9781491415429

 Check out projects, games and lots more at **www.capstonekids.com**